A great figure or physique is nice, but it's self-confidence that makes someone really sexy.

Matmut

LUTTE
ET DISCIPLINES

Technic

58
60
EDEN

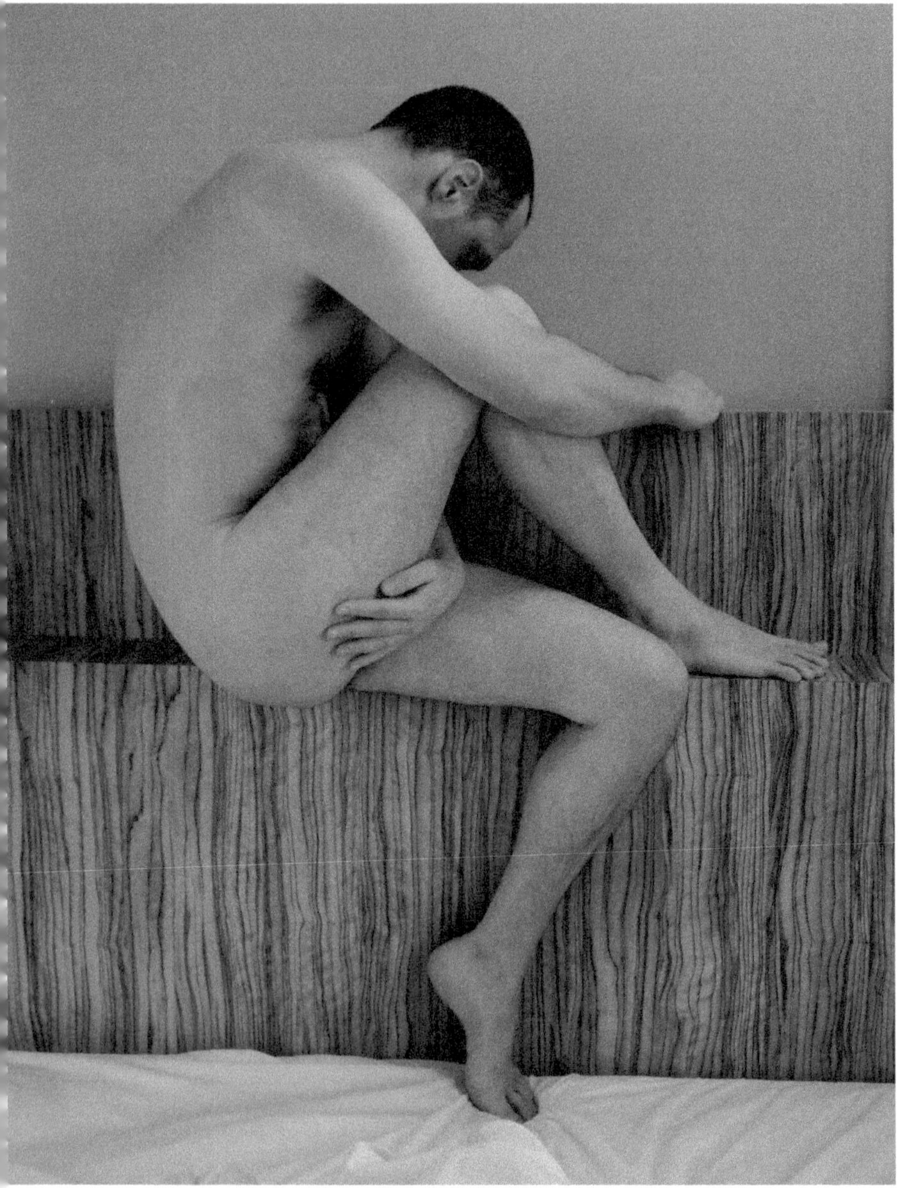

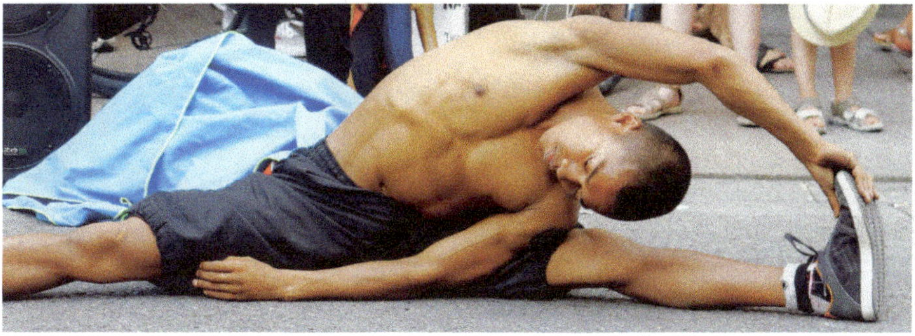

E.Leclerc
ANDREZIEUX

ILIADE

14
FIREX

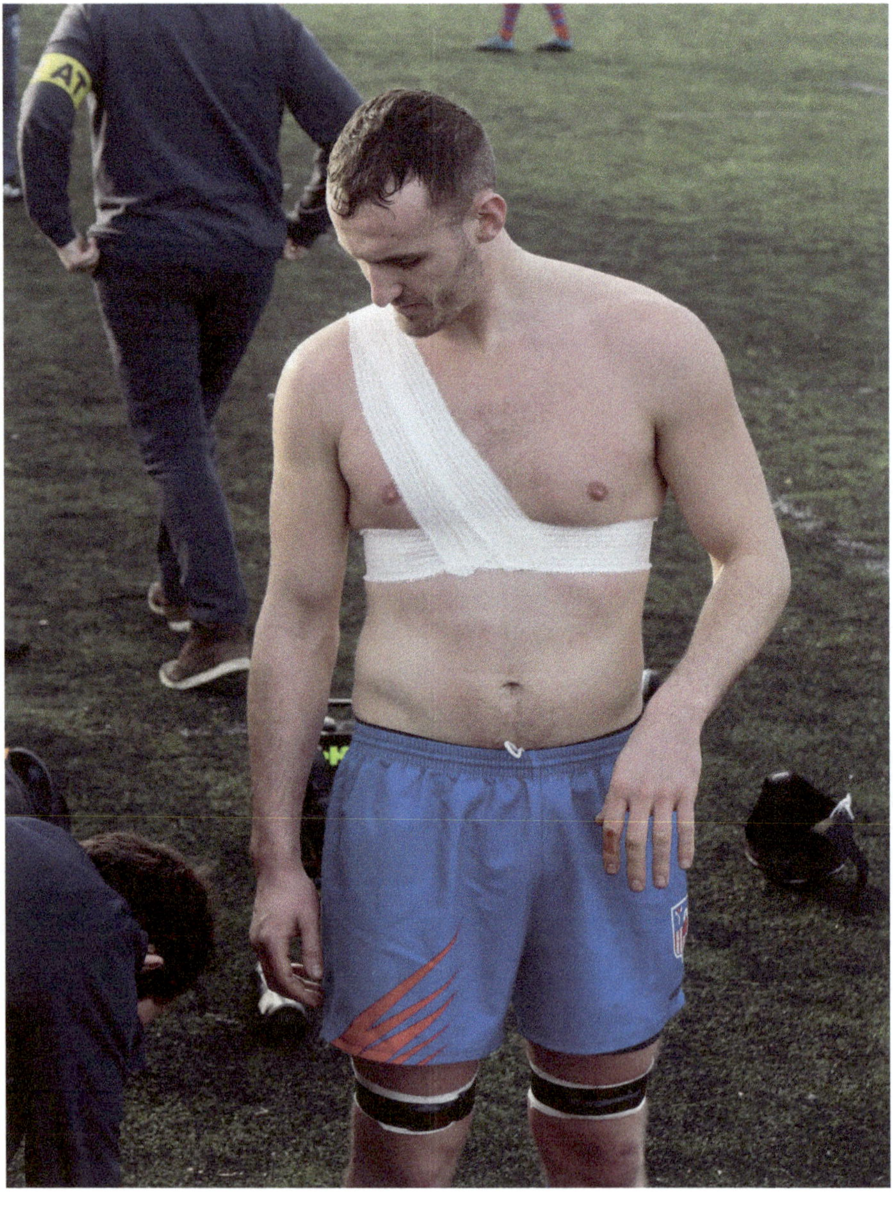

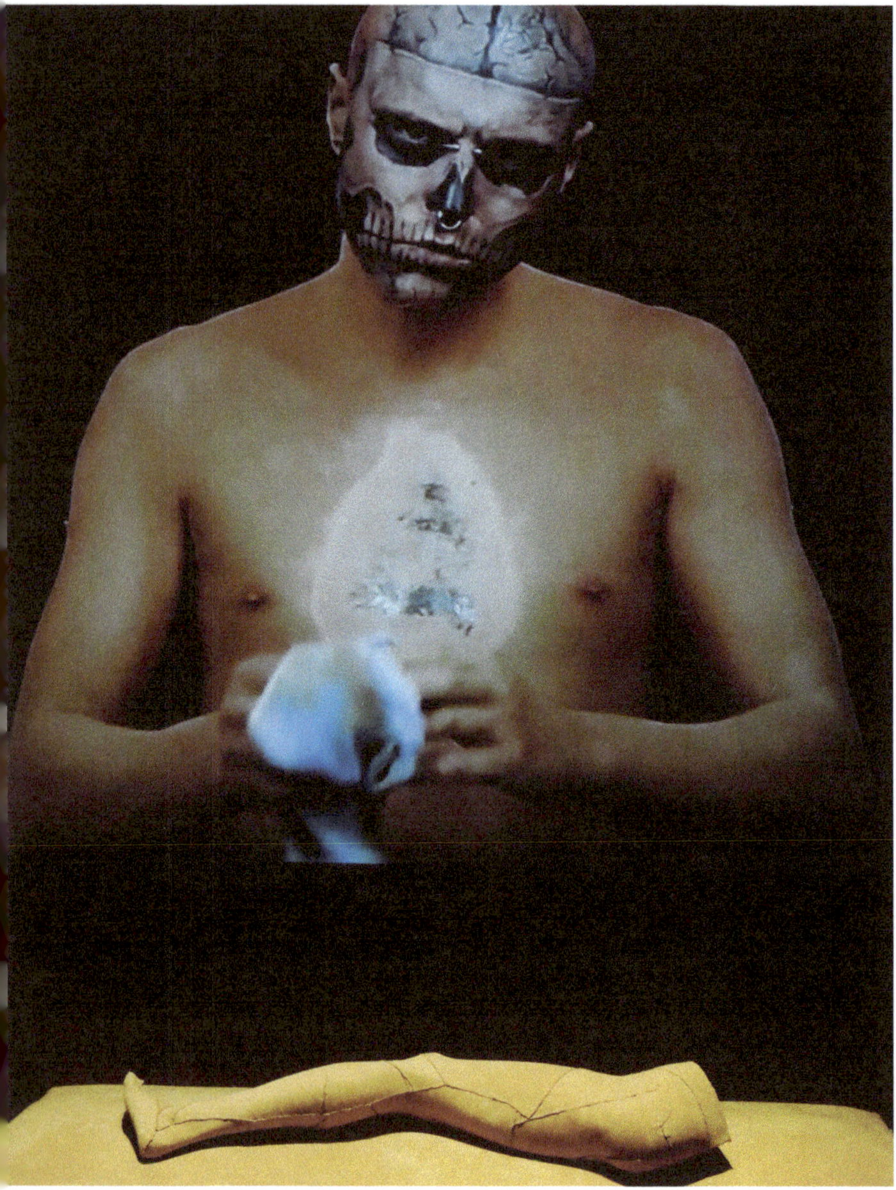

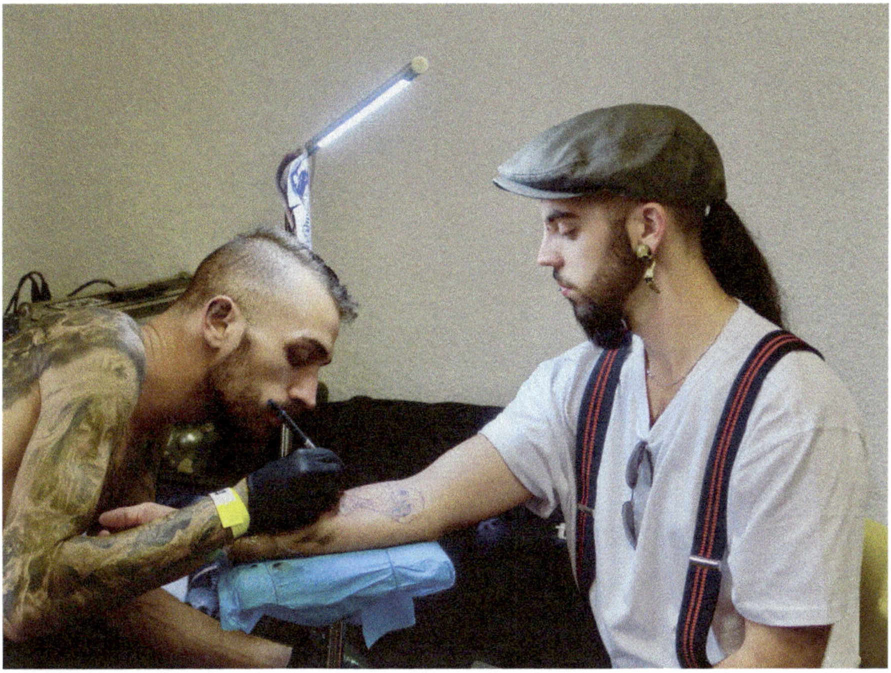

2
5
12
Andréet Fils

ビールセット
キリン一番搾り生
ビール(中)
700円
築地名物
串
海鮮
焼き
どれでも
ひと串
All types, one skewer

14

Oxsitis

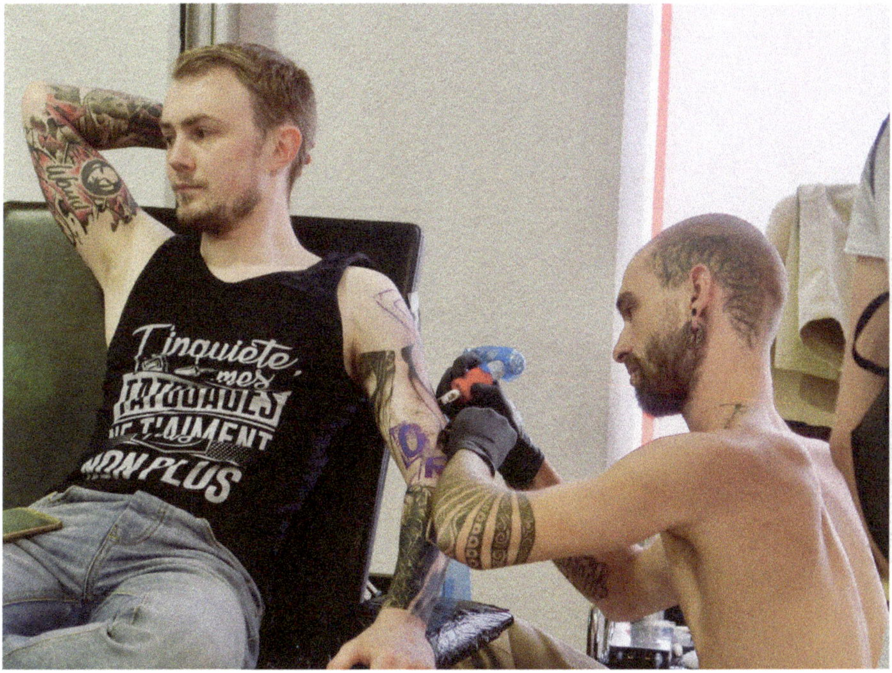
T'inquiète,
mes
T'AIMENT
NON PLUS

SHOP
E SKY

OPALIA
GOMEZ

ILIADE
INGÉNIERIE
ILIADE
INGÉNIERIE

ST
Tél. 04
CORB

GONES
51
17
47

SOCIETE GENERALE

ASSP 69
TRIATHLON
Kalenji
By DECATHLON

Kalenji

CNR

NOU

asics

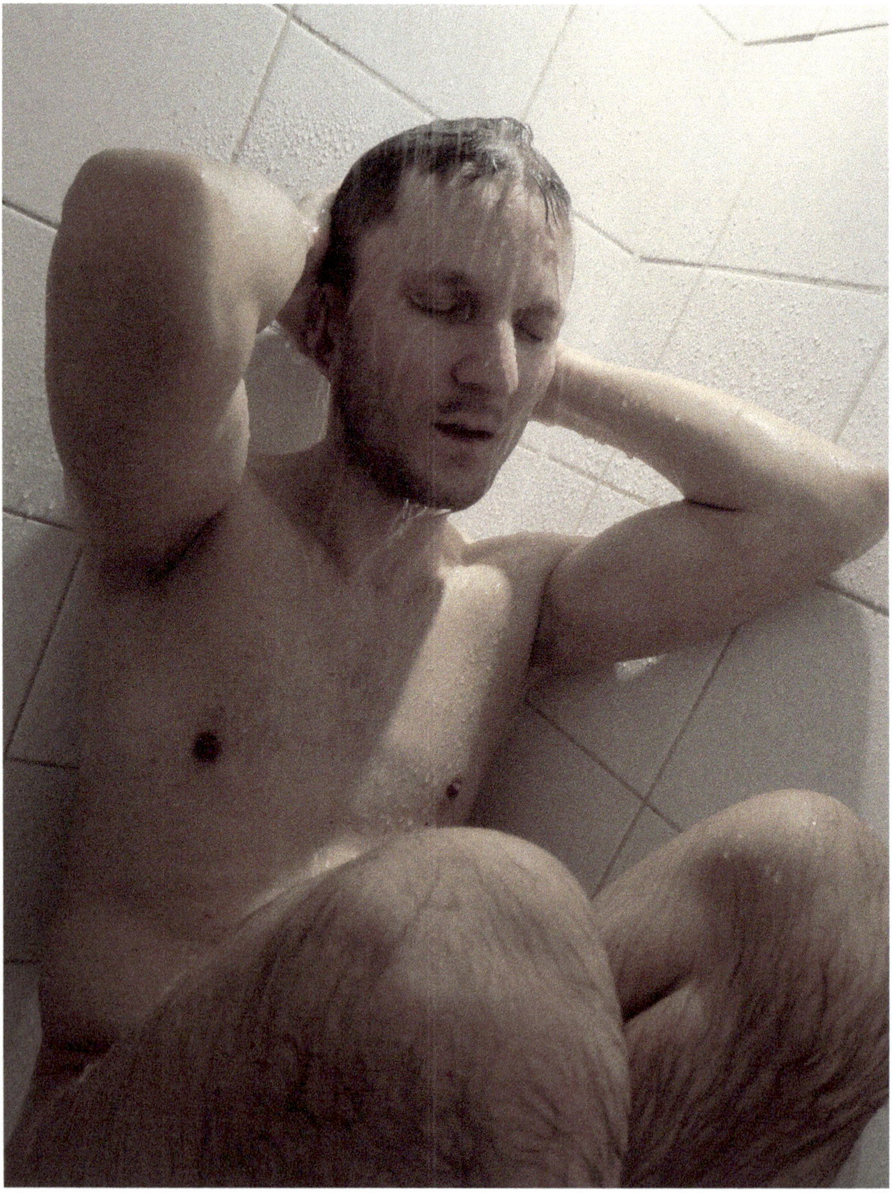

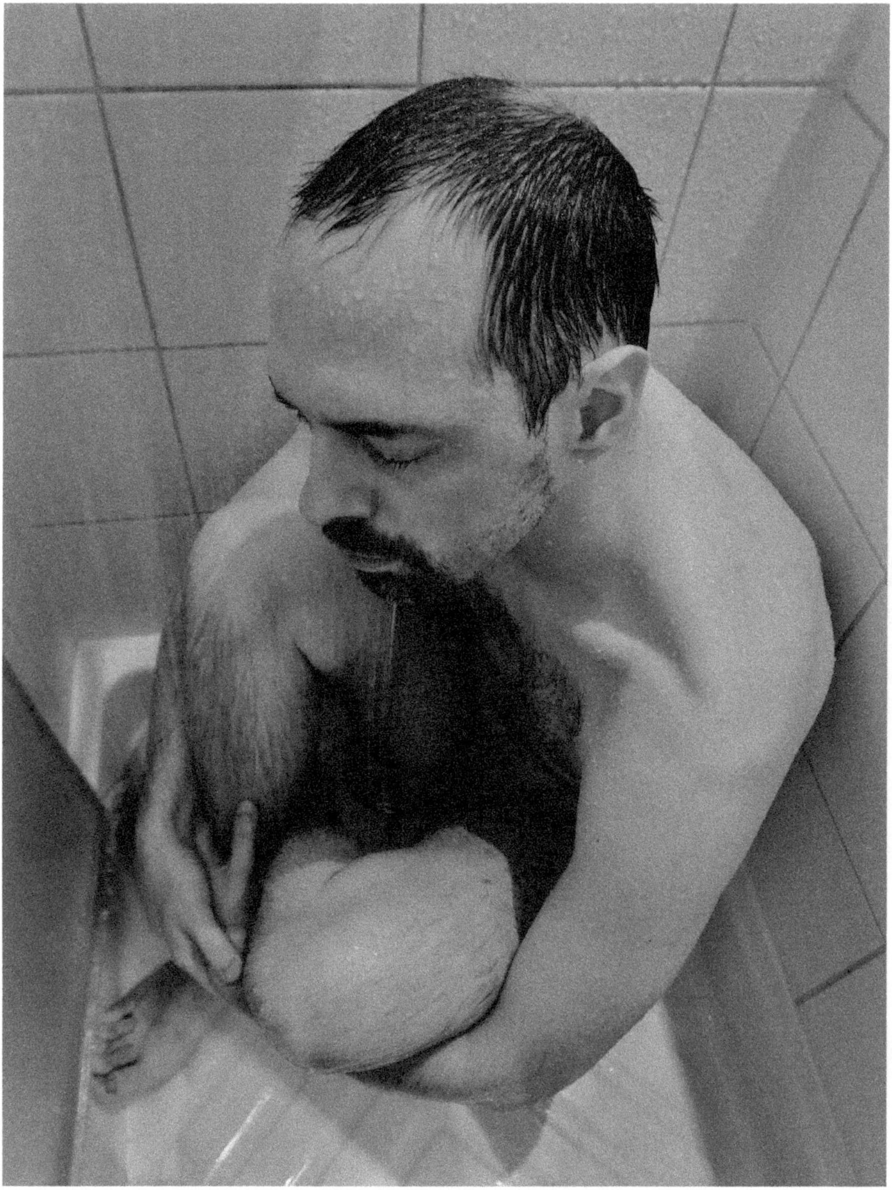

la PISCINE la PISCINE

LES SAUVETEURS EN MER

LA SEYNE SUR MER
PLAGE DES SABLETTES

LAMBERT
TRANSPORTS NATIONAUX
ACTIV'EXPERTISE

MARINES

TAISHAN

FREE

Lightning Source UK Ltd.
Milton Keynes UK
UKHW020157270219
338069UK00002B/66/P

9 780368 317446